FINDING YOUR PATH

A Guide to Life & Happiness
After School

Amba Brown

If I could give one gift, I'd give the knowledge that you're in charge of making your own happiness.

Go out there and create it for yourself.

"The grand essentials
of happiness are:

something to do,
something to love

and something
to hope for."

– George Washington Burnap

Life's a puzzle
of choices.

Remember: some pieces
won't fit, others may
need a change of angle
and some will click
straight in.

Try them out and see
what works for you!

Contents

SCHOOL'S OUT

First and foremost, a huge congratulations is in order for making it this far!

The fact you've opened this book shows you're excited about what's to come. Now that you've done the hard yards, it's time to explore what you want to do with your life (or even just what's right for now).

One of the greatest advantages of this day and age is the range of opportunities at your fingertips. But this also means an overload of information and choice! Not to mention the different pressures from either school or parents. The daunting question: 'What will you do next?' can be extremely stressful when you're racked with indecision and lacking direction.

Typically, up until now, the focus has always been geared towards either getting high grades or simply finishing school, awaiting the next chapter of your life as an adult. It's quite normal to have absolutely no idea what you'll do after school. I've created this guide to inspire you to continually move onwards and upwards and to support you along the way.

Together, we'll work through the facts, creating the framework for you to start making plans. While this book unfortunately can't outline every pathway, I have categorised the key starting points into four chapters. As you read through, you can digest the options of working, travelling, studying or creating your own path. You'll be empowered to make decisions and learn to trust yourself in order to create a path filled with adventure and happiness.

I hope you find this to be a useful tool during your transition into the world after school.

The difference between school and life?

In school, you're taught a lesson and then given a test.

In life, you're given a test that teaches you a lesson.

— Tom Bodett

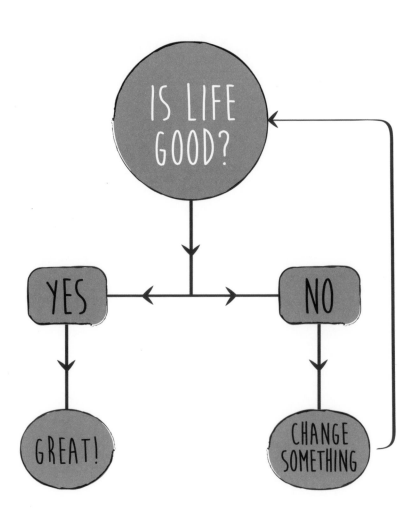

WHILE READING THIS GUIDE

1.

Be mindful.

Keep reflecting on where you're at. Listen to what feels right for you at this point in time. Know where you've been, what you've overcome and what you've achieved. But continue looking ahead and thinking about where you want to go.

2.

Set goals.

What are your short-term goals (daily, weekly, monthly)? What are your long-term goals (1,3,5,10 years)? We'll explore goal-setting tips over the next pages.

3.

Be active.

What steps can you take today that will help you achieve your goals? Everything comes to be by way of the present moment. It's the only thing you can change and the only thing that really exists.

'ON MY WAY TO BEING WELL TRAVELLED'

3 MONTHS = RESEARCHED

6 MONTHS = SAVED $X

1 YEAR = TRAVEL Y

HOW TO SET GOALS

If you're finding it difficult to set clear goals, it may be due to a lack of understanding of your personal values. Your values help to provide the framework for goal setting. They're something you'll be constantly working towards throughout your life; how you want to be as a person.

Values are words that complete the sentence 'I want to be_____'

E.g. I want to be healthy / well travelled / kind / intelligent.

1. Firstly, list as many as you wish.

2. Now, list what you can do (goals) to work towards these values. Write down both short-term and long-term goal posts and set measurable time frames.

E.g. To reach my 'well travelled' value, within three months I will have researched where I'd like to travel. Within six months I will have saved $X and by the end of the year I'll be on a plane travelling to Y.

Set goals you can realistically achieve in the foreseeable future. Achieving a goal will not only give you satisfaction, it will encourage you to set further goals.

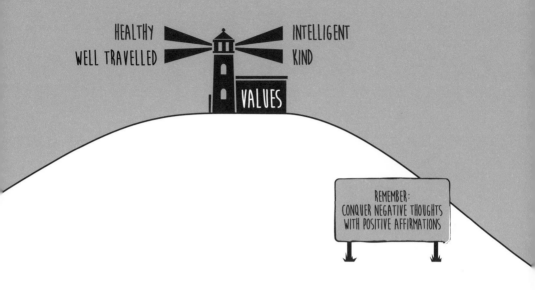

3. After setting your goals, make a separate list of any obstacles you foresee could slow you down or prevent you from reaching them. Be honest with yourself. The way to overcome any obstacle is to name them and identify what you can do, or tell yourself, to overcome them.

E.g. A thought that could arise on your quest to be well travelled is: 'I don't want to have to skip going out with friends to save money'. When this thought comes up I'll remind myself, 'Soon I'll be living it up abroad'. This positive thought challenges the negativity and keeps you on track.

It's not hard to make decisions when you know what your values are.

– Roy E. Disney

PATHWAYS

KEEP LEARNING

EMBRACE A CAUSE

EXPLORE THE WORLD

LISTEN TO YOUR INSTINCT

START YOUR CAREER

LEARN THE ABILITY TO LAUGH AT YOURSELF

TRAVEL OFTEN

TAKE CHANCES

SAY YES MORE OFTEN

FOLLOW YOUR DREAMS

KEEP IN MIND ...

FIND YOUR
OWN WAY

BE A
DOER

MAKE A
DIFFERENCE

You can explore the following pages your own way. You may want to explore just one pathway or chapter, or you can consider them all.

The great thing is each choice holds its own amazing adventure!

Know that nothing is set in stone and it's important to remain open-minded towards opportunities and change along the way. Not everyone gets it right the first go. The answer is often a result of trial and error.

You might not be sure what you want now and that's OK, but the trick is to keep moving. Keep the change happening, and things will stay interesting.

EXPLORE THE WORLD

Chapter 1

How will you explore?

Globetrot

Jet set

Tour

Voyage

Cruise

Vacation

Wander

TRAVEL

If you're still tossing around the thought of taking this path, one thing is for sure – you won't regret it.

If you have no doubts about your decision to travel, get ready for the trip of a lifetime!

When it's time to decide where to go, you'll soon discover there are endless choices. Spend time studying the map for your own local or round-the-world trip. If you are not yet familiar with where the countries are in relation to one another, you'll find this process even more interesting as it all pieces together.

To gain ideas for your adventure and what places best suit your interests, speak with others about where they've been. Research the maps of places you're considering and search for information both online and through travel books.

Think about what activities you'd like to do while you're away. You may be interested in trekking, shopping or spending time relaxing.

Also think about the climates and cultural diversity of possible destinations. Do you want to visit places off the beaten track or tourist hot-spots? Do you want to explore places steeped in history? Are there particular landmarks you've just got to see?

Your choice will of course depend on how much money you can put aside. Don't forget to create a budget and plan how you are going to save? Do you have enough put away or will you have to work after school to save? Once you've saved your pennies and devised your travel plan, you'll be feeling the usual pre-trip travel butterflies made up of nerves and anticipation while you wonder what's ahead!

After feeling as excited as if you're one of the first to set off to explore the world, you'll soon discover there are many travellers just like you, from all over the world.

Above all, remember that no experience is wasted.

The world is a book
and those who do
not travel read
only one page.

– Augustine of Hippo

WHY OVER 900 MILLION PEOPLE TRAVEL AROUND THE GLOBE EVERY YEAR*

Imagine, for a short period of time, you can exist in an alternative universe where you have no responsibilities other than having fun and hunting out new things to see and people to meet.

This will be the kind of universe you'll exist in when you travel.

It's a time to try new things and broaden your mind, tastes and values. The more you try, the more you'll learn about the world and how it makes you feel. As far as you can, without compromise, say yes to more things. Take up the unexpected offers and face the unfamiliar. Be free, party hard, relax to the core, learn and absorb, make friends and be inspired.

Travelling frees you to try new experiences, learn new things and meet new people. Who wouldn't want to experience this?

*Rapport, Nigel: *Social and Cultural Anthropology*: *The Key Concepts*, Third Edition, Routledge New York, 2014

WHY TRAVEL?

DISCOVERY

Travelling is all about discovery. From the minute you arrive at a destination, there are many new sights, sounds, smells, tastes and different customs to take in. By soaking up your new surroundings, participating in the local culture and making new friends you'll not only learn more about the world, but also more about yourself.

Be observant, open-minded and learn to ride the wave that is travel.

In doing this you will stumble upon the most wonderful discoveries.

KNOWLEDGE

Travelling forces you to open your eyes to the world and encourages you to get out of your comfort zone. It teaches you ways to cope with unfamiliar situations, like walking up to a bunch of strangers to make friends, problem solving when you miss a flight or learning to navigate a city when you can't speak the language.

As you gain an understanding of how other people live, your knowledge and perspective of the world is broadened. The lessons learned from travelling are different from those gained in school, or from books or teachers.

PEOPLE

Half of travel's glory can be found in the kind/interesting/adorable/kooky/fun people you meet. So be open to meeting different people and up for making as many friends as possible. Strike up conversations with locals. Go on tours with other travellers. Don't worry about language barriers. You can always use the international language of smiling. For unexplained reasons, smiling is contagious. Give someone a smile and notice how they'll be more open and willing to connect with you.

Some people you may never see again and others could turn into best friends you'll return to visit again and again. No matter whether your friendship is fleeting or everlasting, happiness is always best shared.

Travel is
the only thing
you can buy that is
guaranteed to make
you richer.

SOME IDEAS TO GET YOU THINKING...

EAT A CROISSANT IN **FRANCE**

DRINK A BEER IN **GERMANY**

PRETEND YOU'RE IN A MOVIE IN **NEW YORK**

TAKE A ROAD TRIP IN **AUSTRALIA**

SEE WILD ELEPHANTS IN **AFRICA**

EAT SUSHI IN **JAPAN**

SKY DIVE IN **NEW ZEALAND**

CELEBRATE CHINESE NEW YEAR IN **CHINA**

SEE THE NORTHERN LIGHTS IN **ICELAND**

GO ON A BIKE RIDE IN **COPENHAGEN**

SKINNY DIP IN **BORA BORA**

DANCE IN **RIO DE JANEIRO**

SHOP IN **LONDON**

GO CLUBBING IN **BERLIN**

FALL IN LOVE IN **GREECE**

DRINK VODKA IN **POLAND**

SURF IN **MEXICO**

PARTY UNDER THE FULL MOON IN **THAILAND**

SKI IN **WHISTLER**

VISIT A MARKET IN **MARRAKESH**

EAT GELATO IN **ITALY**

Put down
the map and get
wonderfully lost.

– Unknown

WORKING ABROAD

When you live and work in a place, you get a real sense of the culture, which allows you to discover it like both a local and a foreigner.

Millions of travellers find work overseas by obtaining a visa to work in their country of choice. Once you have a visa, you can either secure a job before jetting off or hunt one out after arriving.

Maybe you have a dream of going to Paris for Fashion Week, Hawaii for a surfing competition or spending a season working on the Swiss snowfields.

Be prepared that turning your dream into reality takes a bit of admin work. You'll need to arrange a visa, book flights and conduct research into all the particulars of working in your country of choice.

You'll also need to find work and accommodation, and sort out everyday necessities, such as a bank account, insurance and a mobile phone. Don't be discouraged. It's completely doable, but can just take a little time.

Working abroad may come with its struggles and frustrations, such as challenges in finding a job, low pay or missing home. However, nothing compares to the highs of knowing you can make a life on the other side of the world – just because you want to.

10 TIPS FOR LIFE-CHANGING TRAVEL

1. *Don't rush.* If you are able, four days in one place should be the minimum: Days 1 and 2 to see the sights everyone's told you about, and days 3 and 4 to make your own discoveries.

2. *Enjoy local dishes.* In every country you visit, make a point of trying the traditional food. Ask a local to recommend places they'd go.

3. *Give yourself time to wander.* After brief research of the areas to avoid and areas of interest, go with a vague direction and no expectations. This is the best way to discover intriguing places and see and experience how the locals live.

4. *Stay in hostels.* Not only are they cheaper than hotels, they also serve as meeting places for making friends and memories. Take the first step to be brave and say hi; the rest will follow naturally.

5. *Research.* The best way to make the most of your time is to research your destination. List activities that interest you, the foods you'd like to try and the places you must visit.

6. *Make sure you find moments to slow down.* Breathe deeply and live in the present. In these moments, you'll really start to appreciate your surroundings and how beautiful life is.

7. *Make an effort to learn the language.* Even if you only learn the basics, the locals will appreciate your effort.

8. *Learn to laugh at yourself.* Know how to make light of annoying situations. Remember: no matter how long the bus ride, how awful the airline food, or how uncomfortable the bed, this moment will not come again.

9. *Take pictures and write a journal.* Capture all of the spectacular, funny and random things you spot along the way and don't want to forget. However small, it's awesome to have a hard copy of the memorable moments.

10. *Two things to make sure you pack and never lose: your passport and an open mind!*

Where will your trip begin?
Trace your journey here...

GLOBETROTTING

I don't know where
I'm going from here,
but I promise
it won't be boring

– David Bowie

GO ON AN ADVENTURE!

It's rare you'll have the opportunity to explore so freely again. Later in life you may have the responsibilities of a career or family, restricting choices and time. So do it now! Travel is a great way to give your mind a rest, have some laughs and become inspired to make a decision about what to do next.

Your options are endless. Whether you want to chase summer or learn about history, get lost in nature or party with others, the world has all this to offer, plus more. Whatever floats your boat, get out there and explore!

KEEP LEARNING

Chapter 2

How will you build your knowledge?

Higher education

Study

University

College

Vocational training

Research after school

Educational institutions

WHY STUDY?

There are no two ways about it – learning as much as you can leads to a more rewarding and fulfilling long-term career.

Regardless of whatever course you choose, after completion you're bound to benefit from greater employment opportunities and a higher salary – not to mention the connections you will make.

Still, traditional education isn't for everyone. A less conventional approach could be actively learning an industry of interest by completing a short course, free online courses or making your own project to gain experience and build your portfolio.

If you're one of the lucky few with a dream career, you'll have more clarity around the decision to study. If this can only be practised with a qualification in hand, then you can be sure study's on your path.

For others, furthering education is a great way to broaden skill sets. If you like the idea of a career, then furthering your education is also a great way to test the waters.

No knowledge learned is ever wasted!

WHAT SHOULD I STUDY?

When deciding what to study, don't place all your focus on working towards a fixed job. It's likely to evolve as you progress. That said, it's still useful to have a broad sense of what you want to do, such as working in the field of science or design.

With some sense of direction, the overall experience of studying will feel more meaningful and worthwhile. That is, you're not just studying for the sake of studying, which can become tiresome and lead to your burning/dropping out.

When you enrol in a course that interests you, specific areas will excite you along the way, ultimately guiding you to a job that is right for you.

Hint: Often we choose paths based on others' success or influence. This is not a long-term plan. Down the track, you'll be more thankful for picking a career of interest.

Where are you at?

Circle what most describes you.

1.
a) I have no idea what course I should apply for.

b) I have a good idea of what subjects I want to learn.

c) I'd prefer to look into other options not related to studying.

2.
a) I enjoy studying no matter what the topic is.

b) I only like studying subjects of interest to me.

c) I want to take a break from study.

3.
a) I'm open to building a career but I don't know what I want to do.

b) I have an end goal of where a course will take me.

c) I'm ready to get into the workforce now.

If you answered:

- Mostly a. Be open to selecting a course that includes subjects that interest you. Over the next few pages we'll go into more detail around this. Don't be disheartened if you still can't pinpoint any specific interests; you could look at doing a broad degree such as a Bachelor of Arts. This will keep your options open and buy you more time to work out your dream job.

- Mostly b. You obviously already have some sort of preference for what to study. You're more likely to benefit from selecting a specific area of study; we just have to finish nutting this out over the next few pages.

- Mostly c. Study probably isn't the right path for you right now. But don't rule it out. You can always take it up later down the line.

THINGS TO CONSIDER

If you've decided to continue to study but you're not sure what to apply for, start by writing down responses to these questions.

Your answers will be useful when deciding what, where and when to study.

What did you receive, or what do you expect to receive, as your final score for finishing high school?
It isn't the be all and end all, but your final score should be considered with reference to the cut-off marks used by universities as a clear-cut way of evaluating which courses you could gain entry to.

What are you good at academically?
List subjects that you've done well in so far. Consider applying for courses that are more weighted towards your academic strengths.

What qualities are you wanting from the school you attend?
Are you seeking a place well known for a particular subject, the overall reputation of the institution or the lectures and tutors employed? What other benefits does it offer? Does it have sporting teams you could join, offer international exchange or assist with work placements?

What costs are you able to outlay for your studies?
Courses differ in their requirements. As a student, you may be expected to outlay money for resources such as art supplies or field trips that are additional to your set fees.

What's the time frame you're able to commit to completing your studies?
Mostly, undergraduate courses take between three to four years to complete full time. Can you imagine yourself continuing on to complete a postgraduate course afterwards? Or, would you prefer to look into shorter (one-year) courses and head out into the workforce sooner rather than later? Before locking into a course, think about your available time frame. (Example: Anyone considering being a doctor should know that the path typically takes around 10 years post–high school.)

What is your preference of study mode?
Do you wish to study full time or part time? By correspondence or face-to-face? Away from home or nearby?

Where is the institution located? Are you willing to move, board on campus or would you prefer an institution where you can commute?
Flexible learning is offered by various institutions for a growing range of subjects. Students are now able to construct their personal balance of study/life/work.

What types of things would you like to learn? What industries or areas interest you?
This question may take a while to answer, but keep at it. Also think about what you wouldn't like to learn (as a means of elimination) and how you'd like to learn. Is your preference exam-based courses, presentations or coursework?

What are your personal strengths and weaknesses?
We all have them. Be honest with yourself. If you're struggling to identify these, ask around to gain insight from others.

What does your dream career look like?
Think big! If you could be anything, what would this be?

WHERE SHOULD I STUDY?

The most common options for study are university, private college or vocational training. Each has its own advantages and opportunities.

Generally speaking, studying at university will be suited to specific industries that require a degree. 'Undergraduate' courses are available to high-school leavers. 'Postgraduate' courses are available once you've completed your undergraduate course and could include a 'Masters', 'PhD/Doctorate' or 'MBA'. Know that many universities around the world offer different payment options.

Private colleges also offer a range of courses and can be a suitable alternative to gaining the accreditation you need. They are generally less competitive, but this can come with higher fees. Some also guarantee employment after completion through their industry contacts, while others may have a strong reputation, strengthening your chances for employment.

Vocational training is often suited to trade-based industries. It is usually a requirement for these jobs and can be completed while working. It can also be a stepping-stone to university if your final high-school marks don't meet the specified criteria.

Whatever you decide
to do, check that
the thought of it
makes you smile.

YOUR APPLICATION

Research

Before making your final decision on which course to apply for, make sure you spend the time researching all the details. The Internet has a near unlimited number of resources with information and advice about the specifics of courses and different careers. A friend or family member working in your field of interest can also be a fantastic resource for understanding what you need to do or achieve to get a similar position. They could act as a great mentor if you need advice or help along the way.

You can also ask your current teachers or school career advisers. Talk to people from the institutions you're thinking of attending. Informal web forums and blog posts give an insight into student opinions, while institutional websites provide the facts. Open Days will give you a sense of the environment and the opportunity to pose any unanswered questions.

Apply

Narrow your choices to a mix of about six to ten courses, where the odds can range from low to high of your gaining admission. Applications should be filled out completely and submitted on time.

If you're struggling, your former school or the institution to which you're applying will be able to offer help or advice.

By taking these positive steps (researching and enrolling in a course), you'll learn more about what interests you and you'll be a few steps closer to knowing where you'd like to go career-wise!

Hint: The process of researching and enrolling in courses also assists in the journey of discovering your future career.

ADVANTAGES OF STUDYING

You get back from life what you put in. For studying, the experience and knowledge you gain are valuable life possessions. Holding a degree/certificate demonstrates personal ability — through your initiative to enrol in a course and your commitment to seeing it through.

There are also long-lasting benefits for your professional life. In comparison with those who haven't studied after high school, you will become more employable, able to demand more money and expand your network. Let's look into these benefits a little further...

1. GET THE JOB YOU WANT

Graduates are often viewed as more motivated, having stronger communication skills, better able to meet deadlines and more able to learn tasks quickly, as this is what's needed to complete your studies. You're also more employable with industry-trained skills and related knowledge.

The fact you have a degree will lower your risk of unemployment and set you above the rest when applying for jobs. The reputation of the school you attend may also increase your competitiveness.

These days, many new jobs are being created to suit new industries born from the rise of IT, increasing the need to have some form of education beyond high school.

Having a qualification won't always mean you'll get a job instantly, but it will put you in good stead for when one comes along!

2. MAKE MORE MONEY

Money is a common motivator for those wanting to pursue study. Although it isn't guaranteed to lead to a higher salary, statistically this is often the case. Higher-paid positions require a deeper level of knowledge, stronger commitment and ambition – all attributes demonstrated in the act of completing a degree.

If you have the drive to complete a course in a field that interests you, and you then have the ambition to continue on the path you set out, you'll succeed.

You'll also be able to major in your field of choice and, typically, specialised jobs will pay higher. For instance, you complete a fashion certificate and during your studies you realise you're best at developing knitwear. You then enrol in another course to strengthen these skills.

Jobs like these are rare, as are the desired people for these positions (those with specific skill sets). If you're the experienced person for the role, when the right job comes along, you'll be the stand-out candidate.

Hint: More money usually equals more responsibility, while more responsibility usually means more experience. If you start with the experience of study from which to work your way up, you'll already be a few steps ahead of the rest.

3. MEET MORE PEOPLE

Meeting new people opens up new possibilities, new experiences, and a world of new knowledge.

You'll find studying far more rewarding if you spend time making friends. Aim to surround yourself with like-minded people. Good networking is a valuable life skill and research shows that learning with people is the best way to absorb information. Meeting people is also key to developing your sense of self, broadening your group of friends and expanding your view on the world.

Starting out at your new school is like starting out anywhere; you'll meet fresh faces in a new environment.

Be open and interested in meeting new people. Everyone's in the same boat, with some having even moved from their home town. These initial strangers, if you make an effort to get to know them, can show you many interesting things about life — how different people are and how varied are their experiences.

This helps you to broaden your mind and enables you to reassess your own values.

The importance of the relationships themselves should also not be overlooked. When working in your later career, your new peers might become good contacts or possibly even colleagues, partners, vendors or customers!

You'll come across people you don't connect with and others you look up to and admire (possibly because of their intelligence or sense of self).

Whatever the experience and whoever the person, meeting new people is invaluable.

*Every person
is a new door
to a different
world*

INTERNATIONAL EXCHANGE

For the adventurous or world-curious types, most universities offer international exchange programmes. This experience is an opportunity beyond all else. It throws you right in the deep end — with a new school, new people, a new country and potentially a new language.

If spending time abroad is something that interests you, make sure you consider the timings and application deadlines to ensure you don't miss out!

You'll find exchanges are usually offered in your first and second years of study as most courses require the completion of specific subjects in the final years before graduation. So when planning, look into your compulsory subjects and how many electives you're able to take. This helps to avoid having to extend your study period.

Hint: You'll learn more about yourself and the world from the awesome highs and lows of studying abroad in 6 months than you would at home in 6 years.

Ever questioned why
birds stay in the same
place when they can
fly anywhere on earth?

Ask yourself this
same question.

I cannot teach
anybody anything.
I can only
make them think.

– Socrates

LISTEN TO YOUR INSTINCT

While completing your studies, embrace the full experience. Be open to new ideas, new people and different ways of learning. The more involved you are, the richer your experience will be. Try hard at making friends, listen in your lectures and choose subjects that genuinely interest you.

While we can never know for sure what the future will hold, if we make decisions by listening to ourselves and being positive, we'll always go in the right direction.

Remember, not everyone has access to such an opportunity. It's a privilege and an accomplishment to continue to study, and a decision that should be respected and enjoyed.

Learning expands your mind; it gives you purpose, aspirations and structure outside of earning a living. However, there are many other roads to take. So if you feel like study isn't for you, don't worry. Simply move on to something else.

START YOUR CAREER

Chapter 3

Things to consider:

Jobs

Employment

Money

Experience

Resumés

Interviews

Organisations

WHY WORK?

Whether you have a direction or not, earning some money and having a well-deserved break from your many years at school might be just what you need to inspire you. This could be the start of working towards a career or financial goal. Either way, being employed equals earning money and gaining experience within the workforce.

Rest assured, being clueless around your career is now the norm for most high-school leavers. Not only are there countless occupations you can choose from, there's also a range of work avenues such as working overseas, working part time or full time, charity work or setting up your own business.

When weighing up possible job choices, speak to people with experience in different fields. If you have an idea of the kind of business you want to be in, start with undertaking some work experience in that area.

Pathways for finding and applying for jobs will vary from online career sites, word of mouth recommendations, adverts in the local paper, different Internet websites to approaching companies directly and asking if they have any opportunities.

Hint: When applying for jobs, your resumé is your tool to sell yourself. This chapter will provide some useful tips for putting together your resumé and also the must-knows for interviewing in order to secure a job.

The best things
in life are free.

The second best
are very expensive

– Coco Chanel

NOTHING BEATS GETTING PAID TO DO WHAT YOU LOVE ... BUT NOTHING'S MORE FRUSTRATING THAN HEARING THIS STATEMENT WHEN YOU HAVEN'T YET FIGURED IT OUT.

While this book can't tell you the answer, it can prompt you to realise it for yourself. Spend some time considering the following questions. Then review your responses and look for the recurring themes.

Do your answers lean more towards indoor or outdoor work? The social services or a design role? Do you enjoy customer service? Would you prefer working individually or in a team? Consider the different related jobs out there while being mindful of your noted interests.

WHAT TO DO FOR WORK?

1. Of all the people I know I would choose to do _____'s job. I would select this because _____ _____.

2. If I had to reselect my electives I would pick _____. I would make this change because _____ _____.

3. I enjoyed _____ at school. I was good at _____ _____ _____.

4. When I have free time, I choose to _____. I like to do this because _____ _____ _____.

5. I have always admired the career of _____. I find this interesting because _____ _____.

6. My friends and family describe me as being very good at _____. because _____ _____ _____.

7. If I could be recognised for or successful at one thing it would be _____ _____.

8. After answering these questions, it seems a common thread of interest is _____ _____ _____.

HOW TO
SEARCH FOR WORK

Hint: When hunting down the job of your dreams, look for as many options in as many places as possible. There are several ways to go about it and it's best not to rely on one avenue. Actively search online, through newspapers, via someone you know or contact companies directly.

ONLINE

A popular starting point is online career sites that can be searched from any country. They list thousands of available jobs, and the application process usually requires the submission of your resumé and a cover letter outlining your abilities and interest in the position. (We'll cover this over the next few pages.)

Jobs listed on these sites receive many applications, so apply for multiple roles that interest you and don't be disheartened if you don't hear back from anyone after several attempts. While many skills are transferable, be conscious not to waste yours or the employers' time by applying for jobs you really don't qualify for.

Print Publications

Check out your newspaper's and magazine's career sections. The application process will be similar in that you'll submit your resumé. These can also be very competitive.

To stand out amongst the rest, directly phone the listed contact to introduce yourself. If there isn't a contact, call the company and ask for the best person to speak to about the advertised role.

Before even seeing your application, they're shown you're keen and capable of being pro-active. When they receive your resumé, they'll be familiar with you and therefore more likely to give you the respect of responding.

Word of mouth

Family and friends are without a doubt the best connection for finding employment. Being recommended for the position automatically makes the process less competitive. Ask around and make it known that you're available and interested in opportunities.

Companies

Many companies don't advertise externally. Instead they'll have a careers section on their website or they may rely on recommendations from other employees/contacts.

To gain a position in a company where you'd like to work, contact them directly. A polite way to go about this is to call and ask whether they have any positions available. If they do, offer to send through your resumé. If they aren't looking, offer anyway. This way they'll have you on file if anything comes up.

PREPARING YOUR RESUMÉ

Your resumé is your tool when applying for jobs. It should summarise your experience and outline why you're the right person for the position.

There are no strict rules for how your resumé must look. One person can have various resumés to use depending on the job they're applying for. Each of us will also have individual preferences for layout and style. Here we'll cover the basics of putting together a resumé, and you can then finish it off with your personal touches.

Hint: Some companies may request you to provide a Curriculum Vitae (CV) instead of a resumé. The basic difference between a resumé and a CV is the length and amount of information included, with a CV being longer and more detailed.

Generally, your resumé should be from one to two pages with the following information:

Personal details

Start with your name at the top of the page, followed by your contact details (address, contact number and email address).

Skills

It's not compulsory, but if you'd like to include your skills, list your strengths and make them relevant and concise.

Education

Provide the year of completion, name/level of certification and the name/location of institution. You may also want to list your grades or details of courses if you believe they're valuable.

Experience

If you've worked before, list your previous jobs in reverse chronological order – that is, newest to oldest. List the employment dates and details, such as the company, position, duties, achievements and skills gained from each experience.

If you haven't worked before, move straight to the additional information section that will showcase your experiences and relevant strengths that make you employable.

Additional information

Extra information you would like to include in your resumé can be listed by using headings such as 'Achievements', 'Courses' or 'Interests'. Only include information you feel is relevant and demonstrates skills or shows part of your personality.

References

Commonly, you will be asked to provide employer references and/ or personal references before being offered a position. It's usually best to have one of each and make sure your referees are informed and prepared to be contacted. In this section you can note: 'References will be available upon request', or include your referee's contact details here.

See sample resumé on pg. 65.

RESUMÉ TIPS!

- Choose a font, style and size that's easy to read and stick to it throughout your resumé. You can also use templates available in Microsoft Word or online, which is even easier than working from scratch.

- Be clear and informative without rambling. Use bullet points and focus on including relevant experience to the role you're applying for.

- List some of your interests to reveal your personality and fit for the company. Some adverts will request a photograph, but typically this is not necessary.

- Mention your achievements – such as the ability to speak another language, sporting achievements, musical talents – and any courses or training you've completed.

- Ensure you spell- and grammar-check your resumé before submitting. Errors in a resumé show lack of care and poor attention to detail. A prospective employer is likely to discount your application based on this alone.

- Attach a cover letter. This is a separate document which summarises briefly but professionally why you're applying and why they should hire you for the role. This is your opportunity to express your eagerness and stand out from your competition. (See example on next page illustrating what to include.)

Cover Letter

Sam Hollan
0422 799 988
samhollan@gmail.com

18 June
Nature Pharmaceuticals

To Hiring Manager
RE: Application for Assistant Position

With reference to the above post on JobsOnline, I would like to express my interest in applying for the position of .... at .... I believe I have the qualities necessary to excel in the role, and that my values are well suited to the company's vision and philosophy.

Attached is my resume, which provides an overview of my academic and employment history. I am confident that I have the relevant skills and experience to be an asset to your company. I would be very pleased to have the opportunity to discuss my application further with you at your convenience.

Please do not hesitate to contact me if you require any additional information.

Thank you for your consideration and I look forward to hearing from you.

Kind Regards

Sam Hollan

Sam Hollan

Resumé

Sam Hollan
47 La Perouse St, Sydney NSW 2000, Australia
0422 799 988 | samhollan@gmail.com

Education
2017
Higher School Certificate
Sydney High School, Sydney, Australia

2015
Year 10 School Certificate

Personal Skills
· Independent worker and strong team member
· Strong written and verbal communication skills
· Self motivated
· Reliable and trustworthy
· Excellent problem solving skills

Computer Skills
· Internet explorer
· MS Suite of Applications
· Data Entry / word processing

Employment History
Jul 2015 – Current
Chemist World, Sydney
Retail Assistant (Part time)

Responsibilities
· Delivery of high-quality customer service as a sales assistant
· Continually develop product knowledge to maintain and increase customer service standards
· Contribute to overall sales
· Resolve customer complaints in a timely and effective manner
· Managing returns, pricing and ticketing stock

March 2015
2 weeks' work experience
Paradise Clothing
Assistant
   Responsibilities
· Serving customers
· Handling cash
· Answering the phone
· General tidying

Achievements
July 2011 – December 2011
International Exchange
Overseas travel to France through school exchange program

Interests
Health, fitness, travel and surfing

References
References will be available upon request.

INTERVIEWING

The next step of the process (after a company matches your resumé to a role) will typically be to attend an interview.

While it's exciting to be offered an interview with a company, it can be extremely daunting, especially if this is your first.

To help you prepare and understand what to expect, here are some tips for before, during and after the interview.

BEFORE THE INTERVIEW

RESEARCH THE COMPANY

Make sure you've researched the company and hold a thorough understanding of who they are and what they do. As a starting point search the company's size, values and history. Any unanswered questions should be kept up your sleeve to ask during the interview.

UNDERSTAND THE ROLE

Also, have a detailed understanding of the role you've applied for. Be clear on why you want this role and why you're the right fit. Some of the most common questions asked include: "Why would you like to undertake this role?", "What strengths or experience do you have that will enable you to do the job?" and "Where do you see yourself in five years' time?"

While you can never be sure what you'll be asked during an interview, if you've researched the company, know what's included in your resumé and have a temporary plan for moving forward, these answers should be mouldable to any question thrown your way.

REHEARSE

Once you know your stuff it's best to practise out loud with another person. Use the varied interview questions available online, including video clips where questions will be asked and you can pause the clip to provide your answer. You can also video your rehearsals to see any bad habits and the overall impression you make.

PLAN WHAT TO WEAR

Prior to the day, also have your interview outfit prepared. Opt for a suit or smart casual clothing with polished shoes, and ensure your nails are manicured, and that your hair is clean and tidy. Presentation plays a large role in first impressions: being well groomed and suitably dressed can reflect your professionalism and ability to represent the company.

BE ON TIME

Aim to be early for your meeting. Punctuality also plays a large role in first impressions. Look up the interview location and plan how you will travel to get there on time. If being late is unavoidable on the day, make sure you politely phone to let them know.

DURING THE INTERVIEW

This is your time to shine. Demonstrate your knowledge and explain your suitability for the role. It's also your chance to ask questions so you can assess if the company /position is right for you.

Nerves

It's normal to feel nervous when being interviewed. Even people who've been interviewed many times can feel this way. Know that the interviewer will expect this and try your best to relax. Being prepared is a great way to boost your confidence and appear committed. If you're super nervous, you can always acknowledge it in a light-hearted way. We're all human.

Ask questions

Asking questions during the interview is a must. It shows that you're interested and engaged. Have about five questions prepared. Take care not to 'take over' the interview with your questions. Just raise them when the conversation naturally allows.

Body language

Be mindful of your body language throughout the interview. Appear professional and engaged by not slouching. Sit upright with your legs together, and look directly at the interviewer.

Answering questions

Answer questions in an informative manner and provide a comprehensive response without rambling. Often you'll be asked behavioural questions at some point in the interview where you're to recall an experience which demonstrated a skill. An example of this would be: 'When was a time you had to work as a team to complete a project?' These questions require quite a bit of information and it can be difficult to structure the response. A good technique for responding to these questions is called the SAO method. The S stands for stating your 'situation', the A stands for explaining the 'action' and the O stands for describing the 'outcome'. By answering in this order you can be confident you will be providing a coherent response.

Ending the interview

At the end of the interview, you'll often be probed to ask questions. Ask any unanswered queries here. If it hasn't yet been explained, ask what the next steps will be and when you can expect to hear the outcome.

Before leaving, thank the interviewer for their time and respectfully shake their hand. Don't forget to keep eye contact to show sincerity and give a smile to convey your gratitude.

WITHIN 24 HOURS OF YOUR INTERVIEW, SEND THE INTERVIEWER A THANK-YOU EMAIL. THIS SHOWS YOUR INTEREST IN THE ROLE AND APPRECIATION FOR THEIR TIME. THEN UNWIND, DISTRACT YOURSELF AND WAIT FOR THE OUTCOME.

GETTING
HANDS-ON EXPERIENCE

It's not always easy to find the perfect job straight out of school. If you have an idea of the kind of job you want to do, unpaid work experience is a great way to get a feel for the industry and understand whether or not it suits you. Chances are, if you're the right fit for the company and a position comes up, you'll be the first person they think to hire.

Initially, it may feel like the benefits aren't worth your free labour; but volunteering your time can really help give you a boost in the right direction. Many industries heavily rely on school-leavers and graduates who are willing to work for free in order to gain experience and make contacts. It's the perfect time to explore different options if you're still living at home, possibly with a part-time job. It's also a great opportunity to demonstrate your worth. It can be a good option for people who feel they don't shine in interviews.

An internship differs from work experience in that it is more structured, like a short-term part-time job. Internships are usually advertised online like any other role, requiring you to submit your resumé and attend an interview if short-listed.

On the other hand, work experience typically relies on you approaching companies and offering to volunteer your time. The amount of time you volunteer is usually negotiated between you and the company.

If you decide to volunteer, look around at companies that interest or inspire you and call them directly to ask if they need a helping hand.

Big or small, there is no harm in asking.

Dedication is the key to success. If you've applied yourself the best you can, then you've succeeded.

ONCE YOU'VE GOT THE JOB

Finding the perfect job is all about trial and error. Only a small portion of us know what career path we want straight out of the gate. Once you've found an industry that excites you, stick to it and give it all you've got!

Some of the paybacks of delving into work after school are not only the money and experience but also expanding your network and acquiring life skills.

Achieving your career goals and succeeding in the professional world is all about proving yourself through hard work and dedication. It's also character building to commit to a role and progress within a company while learning and gaining valuable skills along the way.

Companies appreciate and value loyalty and reward those individuals who prove themselves in their area of work. In certain positions, commitment to the job is regarded just as highly as completing a degree.

If wanting to secure full-time work, make sure it doesn't result in an unbalanced life. Working full time does take up a significant part of your life, which is why it's so important you enjoy the job you choose!

Be realistic. Know there are always parts of a job that won't be favourable. This is all part of life. Remember, you are being paid for your time and efforts and you'll reap rewards from dedicating yourself to a role. Try to take each task in your stride and complete your work to the best of your ability.

The only way to do
great work is to
love what you do.
If you haven't found
it yet, keep looking.
Don't settle.

– Steve Jobs

Choose a job you love,
and you will never
have to work a day
in your life.

– *Confucius*

FINDING YOUR OWN WAY

Chapter 4

What else is there?

Personal projects

Hobbies

Enjoying pastimes

Charity work

Productivity

Get side-tracked

Be a doer

WHAT ELSE COULD YOU DO?

This section of the book is here to sound out the broader life questions and encourage personal growth. It covers helpful tips to kill boredom and make meaningful decisions. Plus, it explores what you could do with your free time, such as beginning your own project, volunteering with a charity or learning a new hobby.

Maybe you'd like to:

- Meet or interact with other people

- Develop a talent or interest

- Help your community

- Solve an existing problem

- Learn a new skill

- Just enjoy yourself

Time may feel endless at the moment, but as you get older it will move faster than you could imagine. So spend your time doing things you believe worthwhile.

Remember, we only get each day once. So live within the moment, as though you won't get it again. Because you won't!

Choosing to develop or work on a project means finding something that provides you with a sense of ambition, accomplishment and fulfilment.

If you start with a small hobby on the side, there's no limit to where it may end up. It could lead into a small business, a new career path or open up a world of new interests and friends.

It is nice to have a little down time after school, following the stress of exams and the final frenzied months. But try not to let this down time linger too long. Between finishing school and deciding on your next step, keep busy with doing things you like. This will keep you more positive and promote your overall happiness.

So get thinking of all of the ideas and possibilities that lie ahead of you and start making them happen, one at a time.

Don't be frozen
with indecision.

PICK A CARD.

LEARN TO
PLAY THE
GUITAR

LEARN TO
SURF

BAKE
CUPCAKES

START
A BLOG

SEW AN
OUTFIT TO
WEAR

KEEP A
DIARY

GO TO A
DANCE
CLASS

ANY CARD!

LEARN
TO KNIT

DRAW A
PICTURE

MAKE ART
USING CLAY

RUN A
MARATHON

WRITE A
STORY

LEARN A
LANGUAGE

START A
BAND WITH
FRIENDS

5 WAYS
TO BE A DOER

1. Believe you have the ability to make something of yourself.

2. Start anywhere and start now; don't wait for the "perfect" time. It will never come.

3. Follow through with your ideas.

4. Don't worry about what others think.

5. If your intention is good, there's no room for regret.

Make
Things
(better)

CREATING A PERSONAL PROJECT

If you're not sure where to begin, simply start with your interests.

Here is a simple exercise to get you started.

 1. **Circle what interests you**

Travel	Film/Video
Decorating	Cultures
Landscaping	Languages
Building	Design
Inventions	Fine art
Children	Photography
Education	Books
Fitness	Creative writing
Sports	Craft
Public speaking	Marketing
Health/Medicine	Space
Environment	Music
Nature	Fashion
Spirituality	Event planning
News	Animals
Counselling	Computers
Psychology	Software
Drama/Dance	Technology
Costuming	
Set Design	

2. Tick why

3. Combine steps 1 & 2 to make your project

To meet people

To assist others

To benefit the environment

To create something

To develop a new skill

To solve an existing problem

To make money

To have fun

You may want to include more than 1 item from each list.

For example:

music + to develop a new skill
= learn how to play the guitar

books + to assist others = volunteer to tutor kids in reading

fashion + marketing & business + to benefit the environment = make jewellery out of recycled materials and sell at a local market

fitness + nature + to have fun = go bushwalking with friends

_____

_____

_____

Life's like riding a bicycle.

To keep your balance, you must keep moving.

– Albert Einstein

CHARITY WORK.
GIVE A LITTLE, GET A LOT.

Another side project you could delve into is volunteer work for charities or not-for-profit organisations. If you have the time, volunteering for a cause you deem worthwhile can be incredibly rewarding.

Choose an area you're passionate about – be it with children, endangered animals, the homeless, a health issue or poverty-stricken community. You might want to volunteer for a charity that supports orphanages, the development of schools in remote areas or work with people in need following the occurrence of a natural disaster. Your time can make a world of difference to those in need.

It could also place you in some confronting and challenging situations. Be prepared and willing to experience hardship first-hand. But these realities help us to grow. Experiencing the quality of life that others endure can definitely make you appreciate your own. It can also inspire you to contribute to making the world a safer, better place.

It's important to contribute to society and do something bigger than yourself. This has been linked to happiness and fulfilment in life.

Create the life you want to live.

Do at least one thing
that makes you proud
every day

GET
SIDE-TRACKED

Don't underestimate the benefits of down time. Through exploring different pastimes you can start to understand more about what you do and don't like, which increases your ability to make decisions. So when the next life choice comes along, you'll find it easier to know the answer.

Same equals same. Do something different from whatever it is you normally turn to. Put down your phone or turn off your TV and go outside and watch the clouds. Go camping with friends. See random movies. Visit galleries and museums. Watch documentaries and listen to podcasts. Spend time with people you love. Drive where you haven't been before and look around.

Experience life in the most hands-on way you can.

Hint: If you're not particularly interested in committing to a hobby or you don't have time to start your own project, try spending your free time doing something different.

PIECING IT TOGETHER

Chapter 5

Let's look at:

Decisions

Questions

Answers

Pathways

Other's tales

Intention

Happiness

In the end, we only
regret the chances
we didn't take,
relationships we were
afraid to have and the
decisions we waited too
long to make.

– Unknown

DECISIONS

When deciding on what to do after school, imagine big things and talk about your dreams. Even if they sound far out. The more you talk about what you want from life, the more likely it will become your reality.

Ask your friends about their plans. Talk about your ideas together.

Ask your parents how they felt after leaving school. Question if and how they knew what they wanted to do. Talk to people who will encourage you, not put you down. Spend time with like-minded people. As the saying goes, 'show me your friends and I'll tell you who you are'.

While taking the next step after school may feel like the biggest decision you've been faced with to date, you'll soon come to realise there is enough time to explore many different possibilities.

Make quick decisions. If something isn't working, change tack. Trust in yourself and your ability to create a life you want to live. After all, we are all responsible for creating and owning our individual happiness.

FINDING HAPPINESS

What is happiness?

Excitement? Peace? A smile?

What we perceive as happiness usually shifts throughout our lives. As a baby, this might be peek-a-boo; in your 20s, it might be going out with friends; and for a retiree, it might be a cup of tea while reading the newspaper. These sorts of simple pleasures could all bring us happiness at different times in life.

In your search, avoid finding happiness purely from others or from material possessions. This may initially make you happy, but it's based on something external and therefore depends on this.

While this external source of happiness, such as a job or a partner, is there, so will be the fear of losing it. Once it is gone, does this take your happiness with it?

The key to true happiness comes from within. It has to be something you feel. It's not for me or anyone to tell you what makes you feel happy. We all have the ability and knowledge within us. Stop and think: what makes you feel happy, sad, interested, down or bored? After you leave school, apply this knowledge to the world and use this information to make the right choices for yourself.

Once you find what makes you happy, make sure you find the time to apply it.

What makes us happy?

It's a tough question when we're all so different.

Often we hear people feel happy from spending time with friends and family, talking to a random person in the street, time alone, seeing someone else happy, singing in the shower, the weather, nature, music, cooking, eating chocolate, Christmas, achieving something, sleeping in or just getting out of bed on a normal day.

How is this relevant to this book? It's important to understand that simply choosing one of these pathways or ticking off a couple of options is not enough. The trick to living a meaningful life is to be able to learn to find happiness in each moment.

Hint: Happiness is a skill. Knowing this means you can strengthen your ability to be happy at any time you decide.

You

can

smile

any~time

you

want.

7 HAPPINESS TRICKS

1. Find activities that you enjoy doing. Things we love to do are our building blocks for happiness.

2. Laugh and smile at least once a day. Even if you don't feel happy. If you smile, your facial muscles can trick your mind into thinking you are!

3. Be kind to others. This is a must for a happy and satisfied life. Acts of kindness have been found to increase our happiness. Spread happiness and positivity to others when you can.

4. Be thankful for the good in your life – even basic things we take for granted, such as food and shelter. What are you grateful for today?

5. Give valuable time and energy to your relationships. Meaningful connections are worth way more than a large number of Facebook friends.

6. Try new things. Add novelty and variety to your life to keep things interesting and to boost happiness.

7. Shift your focus to the positives in your day. By savouring the good things that happen and giving less attention to the bad, you'll automatically be in a better frame of mind!

Hint: Know that we don't have to be happy 24/7. It can be helpful to understand what takes away your happiness and address any causes you can find. Learn to accept the things you can't change and change those you can. Put time aside to have these negative thoughts, but use the rest of your time being proactive in choosing positive ones.

DON'T GIVE UP

Never stop believing you can reach your dreams! For inspiration, look to the many famous people who have been rejected and have failed in the past and now have life stories that serve as motivational tales.

Michael Jordan was cut from his high school basketball teams. Albert Einstein could not speak until the age of four and could not read until the age of seven. Beethoven was called hopeless as a composer, and Doctor Seuss had his first book rejected from 27 publishers. Despite being told they were not good enough, they went on to become some of the most recognised and influential people in history.

Everyone has the capability to succeed. Focus on your goals and dreams and you too can show the world what you're made of.

Your dream doesn't have an expiration date. Take a deep breath and try again.

– Kathy 'KT' Witten

REMEMBER TO GIVE
JUST A SMIDGEN OF
TIME TO SOMETHING
BIGGER
»THAN YOURSELF«

LIFE ♥
& LOVE

CAREER
& WORK

FRIENDS
& FAMILY

THE PATH I PAVED

While I never had one plan in mind, I always knew I wanted to do something random, something I didn't yet know existed. The idea of taking a set path didn't feel enough of a challenge.

With the aim of figuring out what my unknown career could be, I took a year off after school to travel the world. Words can't actually explain how great that trip was; unfortunately I didn't return with any decisions made, except for planning to start uni to buy a little more time.

I selected a broad degree, which allowed me to take different topics. I found myself intrigued with psychology, to the point where I was reading related books in my own time. Before long, I decided to major in psychology and went on to complete my honours in it, as I felt that to be the right progression.

While plodding through my studies, I worked many varied jobs, but none of these felt permanent. They ranged from checkout chick, retail, hospitality, high-end fashion, childcare, recruitment and psychological injury investigations. No two really had anything in common, except the fact that they were opportunities that popped up and were something I hadn't done before. I was open to seeing how I liked them and earned a little cash along the way.

After five years at university and then four years in the workforce, I was fortunate to experience living overseas. Singapore became my home away from home and I can honestly say I wouldn't change it for anything.

Now, with the hindsight of nearly a decade out of school and having experienced first hand all of the different options available (travelling, studying, working and my own personal project), I decided to write this guide for school-leavers to inspire them to continue moving onwards and upwards, even if they don't yet know what to choose as a life plan. Having five younger siblings and being exposed to their concerns over the years has proven to me that the message of this book is still relevant and important. I then realised that contributing to the field of positive psychology was my dream. Writing this book is a personal step towards this.

TALES OF CONTRIBUTED

KRISTEN'S PATH

After school Kristen worked towards her goal of travelling for six months around the globe with a friend. She then completed four years at university, obtaining a Bachelor of Fine Arts, majoring in Textiles.

Through volunteering her time at a textile company while at uni, she was offered a position and spent three years in the workforce. She then took up the opportunity of living abroad in London, where she stayed for two years, also working within the arts field.

Throughout her journey, Kristen learned her passion lies in the development of products and ideas that are useful, beautiful and considerately executed to make the world around her a better place.

Kristen currently works in product development for a rug company that supports Indian weaving traditions and the communities in which its employees live.

SANDE'S PATH

With little idea of what she wanted to do or be, Sande followed the advice of her close family members and completed a broad double degree in Arts and Science, choosing subjects that interested her. This provided a little extra time while she continued to consider where she wanted to go career-wise.

While studying, Sande worked part-time in childcare and spent her holidays travelling to all corners of the globe, opening her eyes to the vast differences between how people live. From America to Europe and various pockets in between, Sande developed what is commonly known as the travel bug.

With her degree under her belt, Sande's love of travel and interest in different cultures fuelled her adventures throughout Asia, where she volunteered in an orphanage in Cambodia.

She then spent time living in Sweden before further travel landed her in Singapore, where she now works as a Project Manager.

THOSE WHO
TO THIS BOOK:

DIANA'S PATH

Following school, Diana, who had grown up in Stockholm, bought a round-the-world ticket and planned to travel for six months. Once she arrived in Australia, however, she loved it so much that she's been residing there ever since.

There Diana fell into the field of Design through a recommendation of a friend, who identified this as Diana's strength.

After studying for three years at a private college, she obtained her Bachelor's degree in Communication Design. She then wrote to the leading design agencies in Sydney seeking employment and landed a Graphic Design position, despite her lack of experience in the field. Diana's talent is demonstrated in the design of this book.

She has since been promoted twice and has undertaken various side projects, including the creation of her own café business, bringing aspects of her own home, Sweden, to Australia. This personal project was achieved with two friends. The passion devoted to her own company is the perfect example of how creating something you love leads to others loving it too.

JAMES'S PATH

James jumped straight into uni after school. He spent two years at his second-preference university before completing his Bachelor of Communications at his preferred, industry-recognised university.

In his final semester, James worked as an intern at Google. Upon completing his degree, he moved to the United States, spending two years snowboarding with friends and managing a restaurant.

He then returned to Australia and started his own business in digital media, before taking a role at an international advertising agency where he spent the next few years. During this time, he collaborated with a bunch of guys to set up a charity initiative to cycle around Australia.

James completed the ride, raising awareness for kids with rare diseases and over one million dollars. He then began working full time at a technology start-up company, which has now turned international. He was offered a position within Asia, where he resides today.

THE ANSWERS

You now have the tools to make your decisions.

Hopefully, after reading through the chapters, one of the pathways will stand out from the rest and you can start to take steps in that direction.

If, like me, the idea of all of these pathways sounds appealing, know there's nothing preventing you from trying them all. Your next question is then, 'Which one first?' This is for you to make a selection based on how you feel when finishing school. Weigh up the pros and cons of each option now that you have the information to do so.

How will you know if your choice is right? Ask yourself this and really listen to the answer. If you can't hear the answer and still don't know, sound it out with others around you or perhaps seek out a mentor.

If, after all of this contemplating, you still have absolutely no idea which way to go first, then just reach for the first one you think of! Once you're done, move on to the next. Before you know it, you'll have explored them all!

They're all worthwhile and I encourage you to try them for yourself. At least that way you'll have your own opinion on each. You'll also really know what you do and don't like doing! So choose the things you like to do and apply them to create the life you want to live – one that brings you happiness.

Sometimes we win
and sometimes
we learn.

NOT TO SPOIL THE
ENDING FOR YOU,
BUT EVERYTHING IS
GOING TO BE *okay.*

Thank you

ACKNOWLEDGEMENTS

*With thanks and admiration to
the beautiful people who gave
their time and love to this book.*

The contribution and efforts of Kristen Masters
enabled me to turn the idea of a book into a reality.
Her input is beyond commendable. In the same
respect, without the talent and generosity of Diana
Chirilas, who designed this book, it would not be
where it is today.

With all my love, I thank James Voltz for the
opportunity and time he allowed me to enjoy being
a writer. His belief in me has kept me going and for
this I am forever grateful.

Endless thanks are also in order to Sande Brown
and my many family members and friends
who continually provided support and
encouragement during the development of
this book. It is undoubtedly full of heart and
wouldn't be so if it weren't for these individuals.

HarperCollins*Publishers*

First published in Australia in 2015
by Finding Your Path Books
Published in 2017
by HarperCollins*Publishers* Australia Pty Limited
ABN 36 009 913 517
harpercollins.com.au

HarperCollins*Publishers*
Level 13, 201 Elizabeth Street, Sydney NSW 2000, Australia
Unit D1, 63 Apollo Drive, Rosedale, Auckland 0632, New Zealand
A 53, Sector 57, Noida, UP, India
1 London Bridge Street, London, SE1 9GF, United Kingdom
2 Bloor Street East, 20th floor, Toronto, Ontario M4W 1A8, Canada
195 Broadway, New York NY 10007, USA

ISBN 978 1 4607 5451 1 (hdbk)
ISBN 978 1 4607 0890 3 (ebook)

Printed and bound in China by RR Donnelley

8 7 6 5 4 3 2 1   17 18 19 20